D0746551

AROUND UXBRIDGE

PAST & PRESENT

PHILIP SHERWOOD

'No society can cut off its deep roots and destroy its history
without forever impoverishing its spirit.'

Kenneth Clark

SUTTON PUBLISHING

Sutton Publishing Limited
Phoenix Mill · Thrupp · Stroud
Gloucestershire · GL5 2BU

First published 2007

Copyright © Philip Sherwood, 2007

Title page photograph: Hillingdon House,
2006.

British Library Cataloguing in Publication Data
A catalogue record for this book is available from the
British Library.

ISBN 978-07509-4794-7

Typeset in 10.5/13.5 Photina.
Typesetting and origination by
Sutton Publishing Limited.
Printed and bound in England.

About the Author

Philip Sherwood is a retired chemist turned local historian who as a Principal Scientific Officer in the Scientific Civil Service has worked for the Transport (formerly Road) Research Laboratory and the Royal Commission on Environmental Pollution. He is a Fellow of the Royal Society of Chemistry, an active member of several amenity and environmental groups, the Publications Editor of the Hayes and Harlington Local History Society and former Chairman of the local branch of the Campaign for the Protection of Rural England. In addition to several technical publications he has compiled several previous publications in the Britain in Old Photographs series. He is also author of *Heathrow: 2000 Years of History* (1999).

CONTENTS

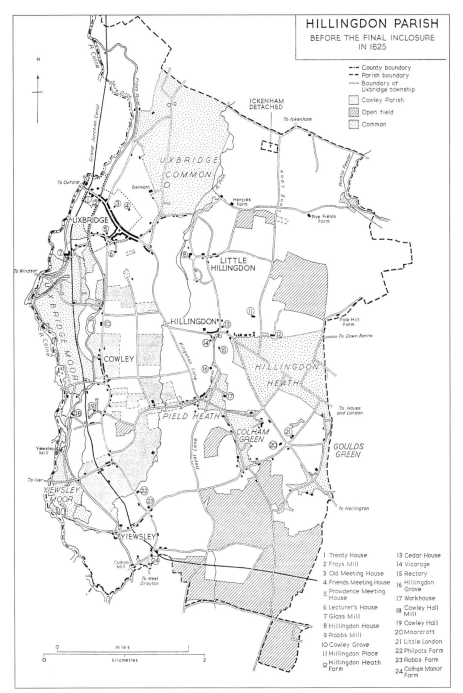

Hillingdon parish before the inclosure of 1825 (*Victoria County History of Middlesex*, vol. 4). This map shows the area covered by the book. Historically Uxbridge lay within the large parish of Hillingdon (which should not be confused with the modern borough with the same name – a modern misnomer). Because of this much of what is thought to be in Uxbridge is strictly speaking in Hillingdon, but an attempt has been made to distinguish the two by including a short section on what is by common consent considered as Hillingdon (not the borough!). For a similar reason Cowley has also been included, because although it is a separate parish it is surrounded on all sides by Hillingdon parish. The three are in fact so closely related that it is difficult to separate them.

INTRODUCTION

In 1800 Uxbridge was one of the most important market towns in Middlesex; close enough to London to serve the city but too far away to be swallowed by it. It had excellent road connections with the capital and was the first stopping point for stage coaches en route from London to Oxford and beyond. Its situation was enhanced by the opening of the Grand Junction (now Grand Union) Canal in 1794, which gave it a further connection with London and soon after to the Midlands. However, unfortunately for the town, it was bypassed by the coming of the

The origins of Uxbridge in Middlesex go back to at least 1107 when it first appears in the records under the name of Woxbrigge. However, in common with many other towns in England, it has a much younger namesake in New England, about 35 miles south-west of Boston. Nor is this the only one: there is also a town named Uxbridge in Ontario, Canada.

Uxbridge, Massachusetts, was founded in 1662 and incorporated as a town in 1727; it currently has a population of just over 11,000. Unlike old Uxbridge it is situated in Worcester County, although there is a Middlesex County in Massachusetts. In 1927 civic leaders of Uxbridge in New England made a visit to Uxbridge in England as part of the bicentenary celebrations held to commemorate the new town's incorporation. The plaque shown here was placed in the newly opened Fassnidge Recreation Ground on this occasion; eighty years later it is still in situ and clearly legible.

railway age when the Great Western Railway from London to the west was routed through West Drayton more than 2 miles to the south. West Drayton station opened in 1838 but a branch line from Uxbridge to the mainline did not appear until 1856, and from then until 1904 this was the only railway link for the town.

In consequence the town declined in importance but it remained the centre for the surrounding villages of West Middlesex and the adjacent Buckinghamshire countryside. However, the buildings lining the High Street had been built for more trade than this – the town at one time had the astonishing total of fifty-four public houses, of which twenty-four were in the High Street (there are now four). Prosperity started to return with the opening of the Metropolitan railway, which gave the town its first direct railway link to London in 1904. The Metropolitan Railway Company actively promoted residential development in West Middlesex by advertising the joys of living in what it called 'Metroland', with pleasant surroundings and a good connection with London by means of its railway line. This had the effect of rapidly urbanising the area between Harrow and Uxbridge and by the outbreak of war in 1939 Uxbridge had become little more than an outer London suburb. To cater for the increase in population Uxbridge once again became an important shopping centre, and during the 1930s several of the old buildings in the High Street were demolished to make way for the new shops that the populace required. Despite this Uxbridge still retained much of the character of an eighteenth-century market town.

The town survived the war substantially intact but it was becoming increasingly apparent that many of the remaining old buildings in the High Street were ill-suited to their purpose. They had been built largely for the passing road traffic and were now expected to cater for a totally different type of trade. The situation was exacerbated by the fact that many of the buildings were wasteful of land, as they occupied a thin frontage on the High Street with a long strip of land behind.

Opposite: Uxbridge and district in 1916 (from the 6in to 1 mile Ordnance Survey map) representing the western half of the area covered by this book. The township of Uxbridge with buildings tightly packed around its High Street is in the north-west corner. It is surrounded on all sides by open land, making it quite distinct from the surrounding villages. To the east are two large areas of parkland representing respectively the grounds of Hillingdon House (page 97) and Hillingdon Court (page 120). Off the map to the south-east and centred on the main road to London is the village of Hillingdon (pages 113–26) and immediately to the south is the village of Cowley (pages 105–12). Uxbridge itself was originally in the large parish of Hillingdon with St Margaret's Church (page 75) being merely a chapel of ease to the mother church of St John (page 117) at the top of Hillingdon Hill. It did not become a separate parish until the nineteenth century; the map gives its area as being 86.581 acres. Hillingdon parish was later further subdivided into two; on this map they are recorded as Hillingdon West, with an acreage of 781.180, and Hillingdon East, which is shown on the map on page 114, with an acreage of 2,954.749.

The name of the modern London Borough of Hillingdon was ill-chosen because it causes so much confusion with the ancient parish of Hillingdon. In fact the borough contains eight other ancient parishes in addition to Hillingdon. Logically Elthorne would have been a much better name, as the borough occupies most of the area of Middlesex that was historically the Hundred of Elthorne.

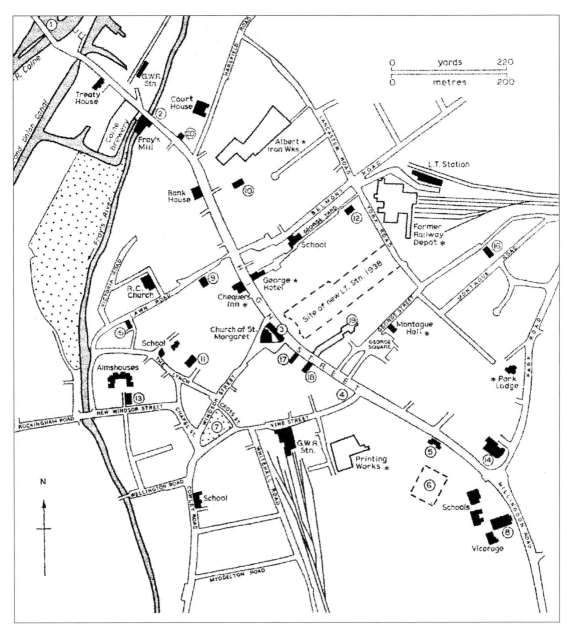

Uxbridge in 1935, based on a map in the *Victoria County History of Middlesex*, vol. 4.

1. High Bridge
2. Fray's or Mercer's Bridge
3. Market House
4. Savoy Cinema*
5. Council Offices*
6. County Buildings & Library*
7. Old Burial Ground
8. St Andrew's Church
9. Former RC Church
10. Old Meeting House
11. Providence Church*

12. Quaker Meeting House
13. Former Methodist Church
14. Methodist Central Hall*
15. Primitive Methodist Chapel
16. Apostolic Church*
17. The Three Tuns
18. The King's Arms
19. Harman's Brewery*
20. The Red House*

* indicates buildings since demolished.

On these strips had been the notorious old yards where many people lived in what had become slums, most of which had largely been demolished in the inter-war years. Clearly something had to be done. The solution put forward by the Council in the 1960s was a massive redevelopment, in which everything in a large segment of the town – the old, the new, the good, the bad and the ugly – would be totally destroyed.

The old properties were replaced with concrete buildings of unbelievable ugliness that, as some of the photographs in this book show, had more than a hint of Communist Eastern Europe about them. Although not alone, Uxbridge was one of the worst examples of this style of redevelopment, succinctly described in 1973 by David McKie in his book *A Sadly Mismanaged Affair*: 'We had seen the character of towns and cities damaged if not destroyed by the vandalistic pulling down of valuable old buildings and the construction of new ones which looked as if they had been taken off the shelf of the developer's warehouse. They bore no relation to the surroundings into which they fitted and were slotted in without distinction into streets of the most sharply differing character.'

The trend begun by the large-scale destruction of the late 1960s and early 1970s has continued until very recently, changing the landscape of the town beyond all recognition. In 1907, exactly 100 years ago, Stephen Springall published his *Country Rambles Around Uxbridge*. The extraordinary opening lines of this book begin: 'Avast! Ye detractors of the beautiful! Avast! If even it be true that the old town of Uxbridge is not an aesthetic town, yet can we with little labour find around Uxbridge an abundance of natural charm to compensate for the lack of town beauty.' If he were still alive today he would have to labour very hard indeed. According to the Bible, Esau sold his inheritance to his brother Jacob for 'a mess of potage', but Uxbridge went one worse and sold its inheritance for a mess. A former Director of Planning of the Council declared on his retirement that he regarded the redevelopment of Uxbridge as his greatest achievement. Sir Arthur (Bomber) Harris no doubt thought the same about what he did to Dresden.

It is hoped that this book, by putting on record what has happened, will remind readers of what has been lost and how important it is to preserve what little remains. In many cases newcomers to the area will have to take my word for it that the before and after photographs really were taken from the same vantage point.

P.T. Sherwood
Harlington, 2007

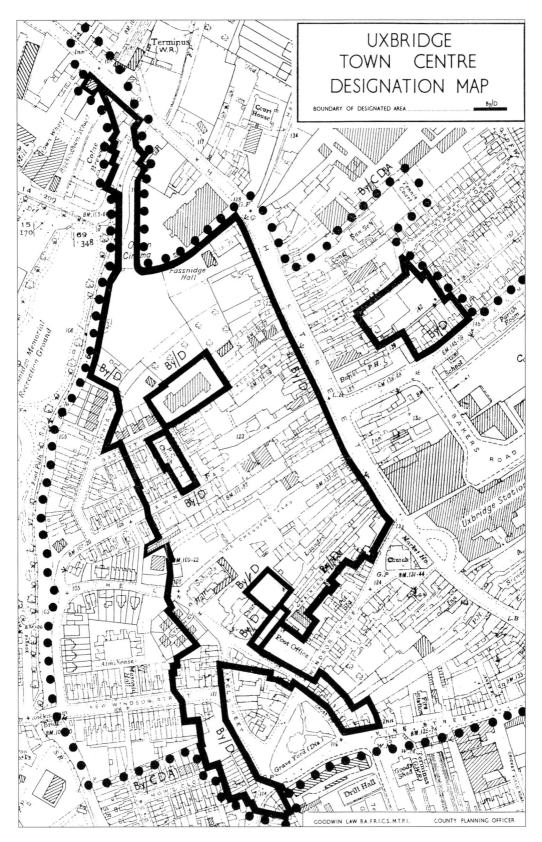

UXBRIDGE
TOWN CENTRE
DESIGNATION MAP

BOUNDARY OF DESIGNATED AREA ....

GOODWIN LAW B.A.,F.R.I.C.S.,M.T.P.I.   COUNTY PLANNING OFFICER

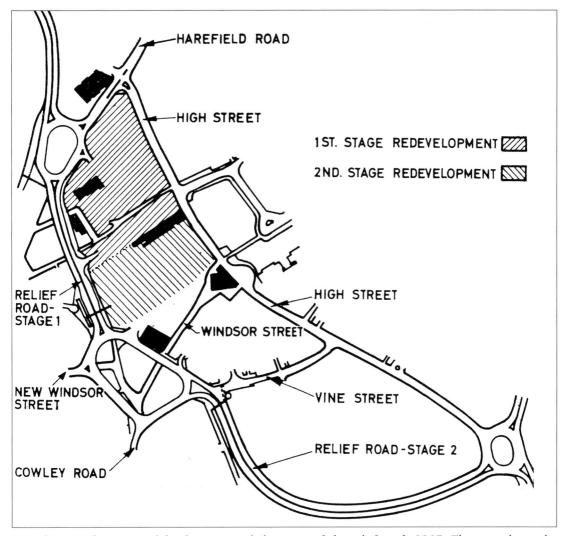

Map showing the stages of development and the route of the relief road, 1967. The map shows the layout of the town after the massive redevelopment of the 1970s. Traffic was diverted from the High Street at a point close to St Andrew's Church (St Andrew's roundabout), with a new road to the west. It converted minor roads such as Cross Street and The Lynch into a new dual-carriageway thoroughfare. The new road then rejoins the Oxford road at the far westerly end of the town. The design was very much in keeping with the 1960s philosophy that traffic could not be expected to adapt to the existing town landscape. Instead the town had to be radically altered so as to make room for the traffic, regardless of the consequences. A comparison of this map with that on page 8 demonstrates that Uxbridge was a classic example of this mindset; few local authorities accepted it with more fervour. *(From 'Civic Affairs' February/March 1967, London Borough of Hillingdon)*

Opposite: This map shows the proposals for the town centre redevelopment of 1963. The dark line shows the area of the redevelopment within which nearly every building was to be demolished; this eventually proved to be the case. With unconscious irony the council claimed that 'A special feature of the proposals is that most of the present buildings along Windsor Street will be retained along with the Market House and St Margaret's Church. This may not satisfy those persons who believe that the opportunity should be taken to make a clean sweep of all old properties while the opportunity presents itself. But it is intended that the buildings thus preserved will serve as a reminder of the old market town atmosphere and provide a contrast with the modern architecture of the new shopping centre.' *(Uxbridge Borough Council)*

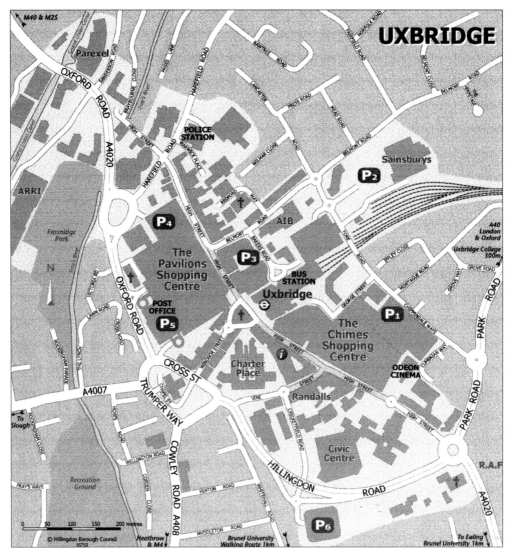

Uxbridge as it is today (2007) after the extensive redevelopments.
(London Borough of Hillingdon)

1
Road Developments

Uxbridge High Street, early 1930s. The road had been designed for horse-drawn traffic and was thus ill-suited to cater for motorised traffic and the inflexible tramway. The first solution to improve traffic flow was therefore the construction of a new road, to be known as Western Avenue, the A40, which would bypass the Uxbridge Road between Shepherds Bush and Denham. Work at the London end of this road began in 1921 and continued throughout the 1920s and 1930s, but it did not reach Denham until 1943. It provided temporary relief but by the mid-1950s, because traffic inevitably expands to fill the space available, it was clear that further action was needed. Unfortunately, as will become all too apparent, the solution adopted by the local authority was worse than the disease. *(K. Pearce)*

Western Avenue looking west, from Hillingdon Circus, 2006. Western Avenue, which bypassed the Uxbridge Road, started at Shepherds Bush and ended at Denham. The road has been widened and provides a direct link to the M40 at Denham; it is usually much busier than this picture suggests.

The relief road under construction, late 1960s. This view shows the devastation caused as the road brutally smashed its way to the west, with Mahjacks Corner at the junction of Windsor Street and what was Chapel Street in the foreground. Spare a thought for the residents in the houses on the left in the middle distance who were cut off from the town centre and whose only access was two pedestrian bridges (built later). *(Uxbridge Library)*

Pedestrian bridge over the relief road looking west, 2006. The remaining bridge of the two that were built to provide access across the relief road. This is the only direct link with the town centre for residents cut off by the Uxbridge Wall – see below.

The Uxbridge Wall, 2006. Unlike Berlin's wall, Uxbridge's wall, which separates the two halves of the town, is still in existence. The photograph shows just how brutally the town was cut in half by the relief road. The concrete buildings across the road from the wall (see upper picture) would certainly not have looked out of place in East Berlin.

The relief road looking east (top) and looking west, from the pedestrian footbridge shown in the previous photograph, 2006. The new road is lined with massive faceless new buildings. St Mary's RC church and the Presbytery, seen in the lower view, are two of the few buildings from the past, but they are overwhelmed by the new developments. A desert has been created where once there was a town. In the far distance of the top view is Cross Street. Compare this scene with the 1967 photographs on the next two pages.

Cross Street looking north from the old burial ground, 1967 and 2006. Cross Street linked Windsor Street with Vine Street, with the old burial ground in the triangle formed by the three roads. Cross Street and Windsor Street were generally acknowledged to be the most attractive part of Uxbridge, with most of the buildings dating back to the eighteenth century or earlier. However, such sentiments carried little weight in the 1960s when all had to be sacrificed to what Margaret Thatcher was later to describe as 'the great car economy'.

Cross Street looking east from Windsor Street, 1967. Halfway along on the left is Turner's antique shop, formerly an inn known as the Catherine Wheel. The sign of the Catherine Wheel can be seen above the shop. An earlier name for the street had been Catherine Wheel Row. All of this was swept away in 1970 to make way for the relief road shown below.

The eastern end of Cross Street at its junction with Vine Street, 1967 and 2006.

High Street/Harefield Road junction, early 1930s and 2006.
All the side roads leading into the High Street were very
narrow. The Alexandra Home for 'delicate girls' (*sic*) on the
left of the junction had to be demolished to provide easier and
safer access. The attractive eighteenth-century building which
survives on the right was at one time the offices of Garners, a
firm of solicitors, but is now the offices of Turbervilles
(formerly Turberville Smith), solicitors and estate agents.
(Old photograph Uxbridge Library)

High Street/Belmont Road junction, 1936 and 2006. This narrow entrance was widened in the 1930s. On the left, then as now, is Barclays Bank; the tall building on the extreme right was the electricity showroom until it was demolished in the early 1980s. The site is now occupied by WH Smith. (*Top photograph Uxbridge Library*)

Hillingdon Road, early 1900s and 2006. Both views are to the west looking down Hillingdon Hill. Until the road was widened in the 1930s this was a single carriageway, which became the 'down' route of the dual carriageway road.

The junction of Hillingdon Road with Kingston Lane looking west towards Uxbridge, early 1900s and 2006. The road leads to Cowley and Colham Green but the finger-post pointing south in the upper photograph points to Harlington and Windsor. To get to either from Uxbridge it would be much better not to start from here!

2

Windsor Street

Mahjacks Corner looking north into Windsor Street, 1991. In the late 1950s Payne's ironmonger's shop in Chapel Street was acquired by Mahjacks (the origin of the name is unknown as the proprietor's name was Edwards). They gradually expanded their business around the corner into the premises that had been Miles Motors in Windsor Street, and opened a timber yard across the road behind the houses in Hows Close. The business became a haven for DIY enthusiasts where customers could poke about at will and friendly advice was always on hand. The business had closed by 1990 and the photograph above was taken just before the premises were demolished – as were the adjoining shops to the north. Windsor Street was cut in half by the relief road and the southern end was completely redeveloped. However, the northern end has survived virtually unscathed and is a pleasant reminder of Uxbridge's past. It is now part of the Old Uxbridge Conservation Area.

Windsor Street/Cross Street, 1970 and 2006. Cowley Road is the main road to West Drayton and the south. It forks right into Vine Street and left into Windsor Street, with the old burial ground in the triangle formed by Vine Street, Windsor Street and Cross Street. The photograph above shows the attractive view that until 1970 travellers from the south would have seen as they entered Windsor Street.

Gateway to the old burial ground, 2006. The burial ground was opened in 1576 as the graveyard for St Margaret's but was closed for burials in 1855. The lower plaque of 1776 and the upper plaque of 1855 on the gateway record these facts. The site survived the wholesale destruction of the 1970s, but its former serenity has been lost for ever.

The whole southern area is now dominated by Capital Court, a modern office block that is not unattractive by the standards of other offices in Uxbridge but is totally out of scale with its surroundings. It now occupies most of the southern end of Windsor Street; it is larger than originally planned. The council has since claimed that it did not realise the building would have such a dominating effect!

Local paper delivery, Staniford's, Windsor Street, *c.* 1970. Staniford's newsagents was the last shop in the block that ran north past Mahjacks (Broome's ironmongers was just around the corner in what was The Lynch). The registration number of the van dates it to 1970 and the woman coming out of the shop is holding a copy of the *Sun* with the headline 'Settle Now' – a sure sign of the strike-prone 1970s. Almost obscured by the van is Uxbridge post office. The Middlesex County Press (formerly King and Hutchings) was the publisher of the local paper at this time.

The former post office building, Windsor Street, 2006. The post office opened in 1909 and closed in 1990 when its business transferred to premises in the newly constructed shopping centre. It was then extended and converted into offices, but the original front façade was mercifully preserved. On the left is the corner of Capital Place, standing close to the site of Staniford's shop in the previous picture. All the shops, of which Staniford's was but one, have been replaced by Capital Place. Northwards from the post office to the High Street the street scene survives, as can be seen in the following photographs.

Windsor Street looking north from Cross Street, 1950s. To the right is the entrance to Cross Street and on the left is the entrance to The Lynch. Ward's shop on the corner of Cross Street has gone but, as can be seen in the lower photograph, everything else has survived.

Windsor Street looking north, 2006.

The northern end of Windsor Street, *c.* 1880 and 2006 The modern view is badly affected by parked cars. Proposals by the council to pedestrianise the street have been fiercely resisted by the shopkeepers, who seem to imagine that all customers park outside their shops and nobody ever arrives on foot.

3

Administration

The former police station, Windsor Street, 2006. The police station opened in 1871 and closed in 1988, when its replacement opened in Harefield Road. It became a restaurant known appropriately as the Old Bill, since renamed the Fig Tree.

Old Court House, Harefield Road, 2006. This attractive Edwardian building, which puts its successor to shame, was opened in 1907. Court proceedings were transferred to the new building in the 1990s.

New Court House, Harefield Road, 2006. This was built on a site immediately to the south of the old court building. Whereas its predecessor had some architectural elegance, the new building is nothing more than a large brick box.

Uxbridge fire station, Cricketfield Road, 1933. Uxbridge has had a fire service of some description since 1770. The volunteer fire brigade that was formed in 1864 later occupied the station seen here. The station closed soon after this photograph was taken, when the brigade moved to new premises that had formerly been the Electric cinema (page 65) in Vine Street. On the outbreak of war in 1939 the fire brigade became part of the Auxiliary Fire Service and

later the Middlesex Fire Brigade (motto: 'Go to Blazes with the Middlesex Fire Brigade'). It is now part of the London Fire Brigade. In 1964 it moved to a new station opposite the junction of Long Lane with the Uxbridge Road in Hillingdon. *(Uxbridge Library)*

Uxbridge Fire Brigade outside their new fire station in Vine Street, 1935. The brigade is setting out to take part in the celebrations for the Silver Jubilee of King George V. Before the days of political correctness the theme 'Dark Town Fire Brigade' and the blackened faces were not considered, nor intended, to be at all offensive. By this time the brigade was fully motorised but the horse-drawn engine had been revived for this special occasion. *(Uxbridge Library)*

The High Street looking north-west from Vine Street, early 1900s. The large building on the extreme left was known as the town hall. This gives a false impression as it had no connection with the local authority; it was privately owned and let out for public functions. It was later converted into the Savoy cinema (page 67). (*Uxbridge Library*)

The Hillingdon end of the High Street looking north-west, early 1900s. The two large Edwardian houses on the left were privately owned at the time but were later acquired by Uxbridge Council and used as office accommodation. They were demolished in the late 1970s to make way for Hillingdon Civic Centre. (*Uxbridge Library*)

Council offices, High Street, early 1970s. Unusually for a town of its size, until the Civic Centre was built Uxbridge had no large central building that functioned as a town hall. Instead its offices were scattered around the town mostly in large houses, as seen here. (*Uxbridge Library*)

Council offices, High Street, early 1980s. These former shops stood next to the King's Arms, which can just be seen on the extreme left. The building on the right was formerly the premises of the Express Dairy, which became the Premier supermarket – the first of its kind in Uxbridge. When the library in the former county buildings was demolished in 1974 its contents were transferred here pending the construction of the new library building on the other side of the King's Arms. It closed when the new library opened in 1988 and has since been demolished. The other building remains and is now (2007) a branch of Lloyds TSB. (*Uxbridge Library*)

Middlesex County Council offices, High Street, 1939. Apart from office accommodation for the county council, the building incorporated a health clinic and a county library. Some of the building survives as part of the Civic Centre into which it was incorporated in the early 1970s. However, the only recognisable feature of the old building is the turret that is now on top of the Civic Centre. *(Uxbridge Library)*

Hillingdon Civic Centre, 1985. The London Borough of Hillingdon was formed by the integration of four previously separate local authorities, each with their own staffs and administrative offices. The decision was taken to bring them together on one site in Uxbridge, and work on the construction began in 1973. The building is unquestionably impressive and it is already listed as being of architectural importance. However, its construction was controversial in view of the immense cost to the local taxpayers. Moreover, internally it is not completely successful: many of the rooms are peculiarly shaped, some have no access to daylight and the acoustics in the committee rooms and council chamber are poor. *(A. Wood)*

A general election meeting outside Uxbridge station, 1955. Charles Curran (1903–72), the Conservative candidate, is standing with the then Prime Minister, Anthony Eden, to his right. Charles Curran, unlike Anthony Eden, was the complete antithesis of the stereotypical Conservative MP. He was selected as the prospective candidate for the Uxbridge constituency in the early 1950s and held regular rumbustious meetings outside Uxbridge station on Saturday evenings that usually attracted a lively crowd. He failed to capture the seat from the sitting Labour MP in 1955 but succeeded at the General Election in 1959. He lost the seat in 1964 but regained it in 1970 and held it up to the time of his death in 1972. (D. Rust)

A by-election meeting, 18 July 1997. John Randall, the Conservative candidate, is standing outside the Turning Point restaurant in Cowley, with his wife Kate and eldest son Peter. The then leader of the opposition William Hague is to his left. The Conservatives had narrowly held the Uxbridge constituency with a majority of 724 in the 1997 General Election, but within a week the MP, Michael Shersby, had died. The resulting by-election was held on 31 July 1997 and was won by local man John Randall with a majority of 3,766. He has held the seat with an increasingly comfortable majority ever since. (J. Randall)

The entrance to the underground bunker of the RAF Operations Room. Just before the outbreak of war in 1939 the decision was taken to build an underground operations room in the grounds of RAF Uxbridge. All RAF aircraft movements in south-east England, including the Battle of Britain, were directed from here.

Battle of Britain Operations Room, 2005. The bunker continued in use after the war but closed in 1958 by which time it had become obsolete. It was restored in 1975 and has become a museum, which in 2006 attracted more than 6,000 visitors. When the Civic Centre was built in the early 1970s Uxbridge acquired another underground bunker, 12ft below ground and equipped to deal with major catastrophic incidents. With the passing of the Cold War this too became obsolete, and it is now used for storing the council's files. *(N. Catford)*

4

Trade & Industry

Lowe and Shawyer's nursery, *c.* 1920. The nursery was founded by Joseph Lowe in 1868 and stood between Kingston Lane and Cowley Road. At its zenith it was some 200 acres in extent and was the largest for cut flowers in the country. It went into voluntary liquidation in 1958 and its site is now occupied by Brunel University. This photograph was probably taken for publicity purposes as the young women seem too well dressed for nursery work. The woman in the centre is Dorothy Robinson; the others are unknown. *(M. Sherwood)*

Barclays Bank, 1967. The bank occupies a prominent position on the corner of the High Street with Belmont Road. The building dates from 1791, but only the façade is original as it was gutted and rebuilt in 1975. If the changes been made ten years earlier it would have probably been demolished, like the buildings opposite.

Old Bank House, 1967. Old Bank House together with The Cedars (page 99) and the premises seen on the extreme left were the only three on this side of the High Street to escape the devastation of the late 1960s. It dates from the late eighteenth century and, as its name suggests, was originally a bank. For most of the twentieth century it was the premises of Turberville Smith, a local firm of solicitors, but latterly has been used as offices by Hillingdon Council.

The garden of Old Bank House, 1965. The garden at the rear of Old Bank House adjoined that of The Cedars; they both stretched down to the River Frays. Most of the garden was lost when the relief road was cut through in the late 1960s. Only a small fragment remains, separated from the river by the relief road. *(Uxbridge Library)*

The garden of Old Bank House from a Pavilions car park, 2006. At least some of the garden survives, which is more than can be said of the garden of The Cedars – which was just beyond the greenery in the foreground (page 101).

The former premises of the Westminster Bank, High Street, 1984. This late Victorian building stood next to the Savoy cinema and was demolished with it at the same time. By the standards of the time it was a rather modest building for a bank, but not unattractive. The bank merged with the National Provincial Bank, which had a branch almost opposite, in 1968, the new bank becoming the National Westminster (NatWest) Bank. The NatWest is now owned by the Royal Bank of Scotland, which by pure coincidence has its own premises very close by, on the site of the Savoy cinema. (A.G. Wood)

The NatWest, The Pavilions, 2006. Banks at one time went out of their way to have impressive premises so as to give an appearance of permanence and stability. Barclays Bank and the Old Bank House (page 40) are good examples of this. They now try to project a more welcoming and friendly image, but the bank has failed lamentably with this branch. The front looks more like the entrance to a public convenience than to a bank.

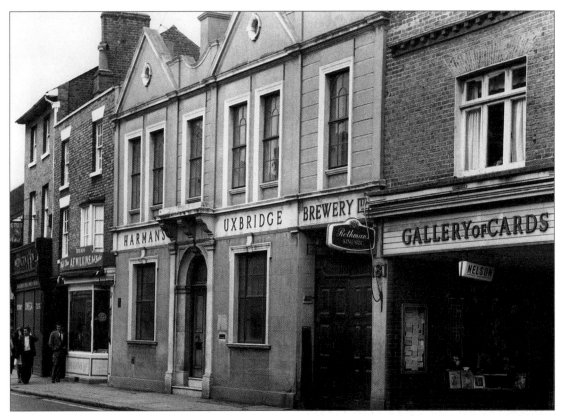

Offices of Harman's Brewery, High Street, 1967. The business was founded by George Harman in 1763 and moved to premises in the High Street in 1875, where it remained until it was sold to Courage's Brewery in 1962. Courage closed the brewery in 1964 and the premises were demolished soon after the photograph was taken. Budgen's supermarket (which later became a shop called Madhouse) opened on the site but this building was in turn demolished to make way for The Chimes in the late 1990s. The shops (or at least their frontages) to the left of the picture remain and the site of the offices is currently occupied (2007) by Books Etc.

Harman's Brewery from George Street, 1967. The buildings were still standing but had been empty for three years; they were demolished soon afterwards. Harman House now occupies the site.

Harman House, Chippendale Way, 2006. This office block, which sadly is not the ugliest building in Uxbridge, was opened in 1985. It is named after Harman's Brewery which stood nearby, although it is doubtful if George Harman, the founder of the brewery, would appreciate the connection.

Although small on a national scale, Harman's Brewery was a major local player with a presence in most of the towns and villages within a 10-mile radius of Uxbridge. This picture is of the King William IV in Sipson when it was still a Harman's house. Like most Harman's pubs it subsequently became a Courage house but is now part of the Greene King chain. Dating from the sixteenth century, and with a Grade II listing, it is threatened with demolition as part of the proposed expansion of Heathrow Airport.

Randalls old and new, Vine Street, 1935. Randalls was established in 1891 and is still going strong with the former managing director now the local MP (page 37). This photograph shows their old premises with the new premises under construction on an adjoining site. When the business transferred to the new shop the old building was demolished. *(Uxbridge Library)*

Randall's stores, Vine Street, 2006. Apart from a later extension and the sad disappearance of the clock, the building has not changed in the past seventy years. Although purpose-built as a departmental store it is a building typical of its time, and could easily be mistaken for a conversion from a 1930s cinema.

Two views of Rayner's pharmacy, High Street, early 1960s. William Rayner founded the business in the early nineteenth century and it continued to operate from here until it closed in 1962. Although fully able to compete with modern developments, the shop traded on its nineteenth-century image and provided a fascinating glimpse of an age when pharmacists (who called themselves chemists and still do – although very few of them are) dispensed their own potions. The shop and all the adjoining buildings disappeared in the general redevelopment of the area, but the fine Georgian shopfront was rescued by the London Museum. (*Uxbridge Library*)

The south-west side of the High Street, mid-1950s. The view is to the east with the market house in the distance. *(Uxbridge Library)*

The same view just before completion of the rebuilding, 1973. Every building fronting the High Street between Windsor Street and the building that can just be seen on the extreme right, together with the whole of the area behind them, was flattened to make way for the new development, with the result that can be seen here. *(Uxbridge Library)*

The Pavilions shopping precinct from the High Street, 2006. In an attempt to soften the harshness of the concrete exterior, which has weathered very badly, trees have been planted and some of the tower blocks reclad. However, in less than twenty years two of the tower blocks had become derelict; they were still standing empty in 2006.

Market Square in the precinct, 1981. The new precinct was a depressing affair. It was open to the elements and always seemed cold and draughty even on a summer's day. Far from enticing people of the surrounding area to visit Uxbridge to do their shopping it drove them to other more attractive shopping centres, which they could reach just as easily. *(Uxbridge Library)*

Shopping precinct looking towards Chequers Square, 1978. *(Uxbridge Library)*

Conversion of the shopping precinct to The Pavilions Shopping Mall, 1986. Because the original shopping precinct had failed to attract custom, it became obvious that something had to be done to make it independent of the weather. The solution adopted was to cover the open areas with a glass roof. (*A.G. Wood*)

Site of The Chequers (Peacock) public house, 1983. The plans for the shopping precinct included a pub, originally known as The Peacock, in one of the two main squares, but the design was fundamentally flawed and it never proved to be a popular venue. It also attracted the wrong type of clientele, thereby gaining a bad reputation. In an attempt to improve the situation it was placed under new management and renamed The Chequers. Unfortunately it remained unpopular and the redevelopment of the precinct involved its demolition; it was replaced by the café seen in the next photograph. (*A.G. Wood*)

Café in Chequers Square, 2006. The square is named after the old coaching inn that stood in the High Street, close to where Marks and Spencers is today.

The Pavilions shopping mall looking towards Chequers Square, 2006. A comparison of this view with earlier photographs of the precinct shows that the designers remarkably managed to make a silk purse out of a sow's ear. Unfortunately it has proved more difficult to improve the exterior.

Gilles's shop, 59 High Street, late 1940s. The Gilles family were from Sheffield and their shop in the High Street was opened by William Gilles (1821–1904) in 1852. It continued in the family for three generations (they were all named William) until it closed in 1954. On the brickwork is something that looks suspiciously like graffiti, almost unknown at that time but a clear indication that the writing was already on the wall for what has since become a serious problem. On closure the shop became yet another branch of Kirby Brothers, continuing as such until it was demolished in 1968. (*Uxbridge Library*)

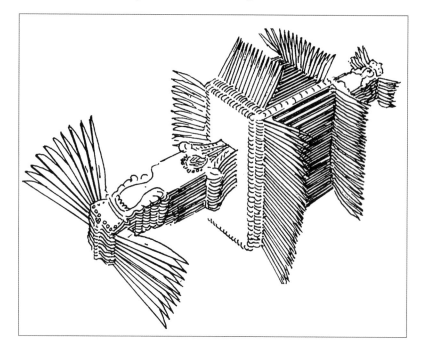

The Gilles knife (based on a drawing by Arthur Jones in *An Uxbridge Sketchbook*, 1977). In the window of the shop was a knife with 366 blades (one for every day of the year and one for leap year), made as an example of the cutler's art. This was an attraction for small boys: it was rumoured that if they could open and close the knife without cutting themselves they could have it. The knife is now on display in Uxbridge Library.

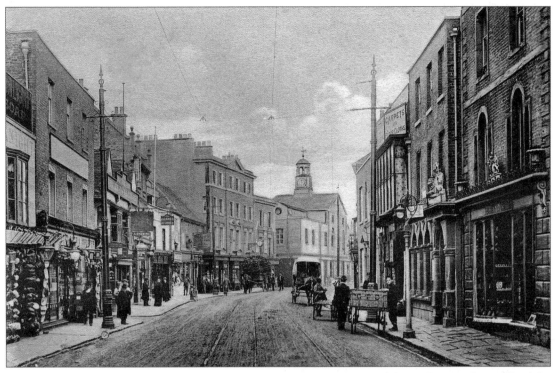

High Street east of the market house, early 1900s and 2006. This part of the High Street has suffered far less from insensitive redevelopments and many of the old buildings in the earlier photograph can be easily identified in the one from 100 years later. In the background of both views is the market house. It was built in 1788 on the same site as an earlier market house dating from 1561. *(Top photograph Uxbridge Library)*

High Street to the east of the previous views, 1990 and 2006. Burge and Gall's furniture shop and the adjoining charity shop were demolished soon after the earlier photograph was taken. Although they had been badly mutilated over the years they proved to be much older than had been realised, with features from the fifteenth century. They were replaced with the new building for Uxbridge Library, which although of rather bland appearance does not detract from the older buildings on either side.

The north-east side of the High Street, 1930s and 2006. This side of the High Street between Belmont Road and Harefield Road has largely survived, with the regrettable intrusion of the building now occupied by McDonalds. To be fair to them, although they have done nothing to improve the façade they were not the first to occupy the shop – which was built in the late 1930s and was one of several in the High Street occupied by Kirby Brothers. *(Top photograph Uxbridge Library)*

Kirby Brothers' shop on the north-west side of the High Street, 1950. Kirby Brothers was a firm of builders merchants which was founded, according to the plaque above this shop, in 1912. It was one of a parade (which also included The George, page 91) that occupied the area between Woolworths and Belmont Road. *(Uxbridge Library)*

High Street, 2006. These shops occupy the site of (among others) Kirby's shop (above) and the George Hotel (page 91).

Another of Kirby's shops in the High Street during its renovation in 1978. The renovation revealed a late Georgian front complete with wrought ironwork which had previously been partially obscured. Because of the plethora of Kirby's shops in the High Street it was difficult to decide which stocked the particular item one required. *(D. Edwards)*

The same shop in 2006. The building dates from the mid-eighteenth century and like many of the adjoining properties has a Grade II listing.

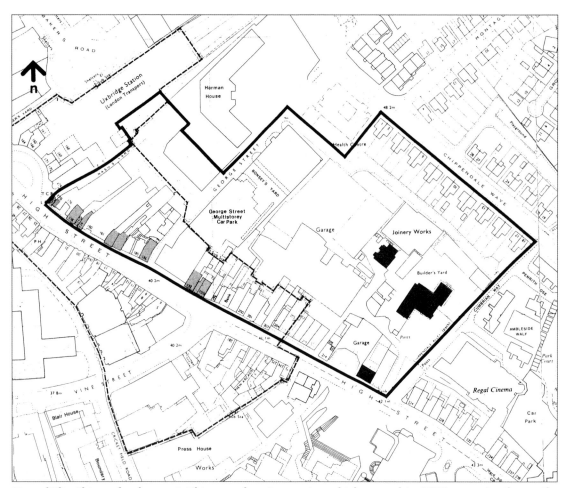

Map of The Chimes development. This new shopping centre, which opened in 2001, occupies the north-west side of the High Street between the underground station and what had been the Regal cinema and is now a nightclub (page 66). The St George's Centre was the intended name of the development but this was abandoned when the name was given to a shopping centre at nearby Harrow. The name eventually chosen was said to be based on the chimes of the nearby market house which 'chimed' (although tolled would be a more accurate description) to announce the opening of the market. Along this part of the High Street frontage were many old buildings well worthy of preservation but intermingled with later shoddy developments that did little to enhance the scene. According to its sponsors, 'The Chimes integrates fully with its surroundings; particular care was taken to ensure that the design of the shopping centre reflected the scale of the existing High Street which forms part of the conservation area and contains listed buildings. The Chimes has provided a blend of the old with the new, successfully preserving and re-using existing buildings while providing modern shopping facilities.' The following photographs show that it is difficult to argue with this, and the development provided a welcome contrast to the Pavilions. Clearly today's councillors and the officers in the planning department had realised the enormity of the blunders made by their predecessors. *(London Borough of Hillingdon)*

The interior of The Chimes, 2006. The development has brought many well-known High Street names to Uxbridge and includes a nine-screen cinema. This and the redevelopment of The Pavilions has done much to revivify Uxbridge as a shopping centre after the disastrous development of the 1970s.

The High Street from the LT station, 1993 and just before The Chimes redevelopment. Many of the buildings dated from the eighteenth century but in between were later unfortunate intrusions such as Ketts on the extreme left and the supermarket in the middle distance, which had been built on the site of Harman's Brewery (page 43).

High Street after redevelopment, 2006. The best of the buildings, or at least their façades, have been retained, and the remainder replaced by frontages more in keeping with their surroundings.

The High Street before and after The Chimes, 1993 and 2006.

The Shrubbery, *c*. 1950. This early nineteenth-century town house had become the offices of Fassnidge (later Fassnidge, Son and Norris), a firm of local builders. It stands on the edge of The Chimes and was refurbished as a part of this project. (*Uxbridge Library*)

Opposite: The Shrubbery, now a branch of Pizza Hut, 2006. The building has been carefully restored and survives intact, but the half-timbered building to its right is a well-executed modern fake. It was built using some of the timbers preserved from several Uxbridge buildings demolished in previous redevelopments.

Rear of The Chimes, Chippendale Way 2006. The Chimes occupies the whole area between the High Street and Chippendale Way. The view here is of the car park, which compares favourably with the Pavilions car parks seen in earlier photographs. However, all is not as it may seem. Before the car park was built Chippendale Way was a single carriage-way residential road: the houses on the southern side were demolished to make way for road widening and the construction of the car park.

Houses on the north side of Chippendale Way, 2006. Houses similar to these occupied the south side of the road before they were demolished to make way for The Chimes.

5

Leisure & Entertainment

The Empire Electric cinema, Vine Street, shortly after closure. This was the first
purpose-built cinema to open in the area. It began life as the Empire cinema in 1910
but within a year had become the Empire Electric theatre. It continued until 1929 but
its trade suffered when the nearby Savoy cinema (page 67) opened in 1921.
The building was converted to a fire station in 1933 and continued in use until the
brigade was transferred to a new station in Hillingdon. It then became a youth centre,
but was later demolished and replaced with a large office block.

The former RAF cinema, 2006. The RAF cinema was built on the corner of the camp in 1918 close to the main road and almost opposite St Andrew's church (the spire of which can be seen in the background). It was initially used as a lecture hall for instructing new recruits to the RAF but soon became open to the public not only as a cinema but also for concerts and other public functions. By 1927 it was in full-time use as a cinema and continued as such until it closed on the outbreak of war in 1939. It re-opened after the war but more as a theatre for local groups than a cinema. The building has not been used for many years and today is semi-derelict.

The former Regal cinema, High Street, 1982. This cinema opened for custom on Boxing Day in 1931 and closed on 4 December 1977. At the time that this photograph was taken it had been standing empty for five years, but had been saved from demolition: just before its closure it had been granted Grade II listed status on account of its fine Art Deco interior. The narrow frontage to the High Street belied the size of what lay behind; apart from the vast auditorium it also included a large foyer, a tea room and a dance hall. It reopened as a snooker hall in 1984 and later became a nightclub. It has been empty since 2006 and its future use is uncertain.

Former Savoy cinema, Vine Street corner, 1982. The Savoy cinema, which opened for business in 1921, was a conversion of the building that had been the town hall (page 34). The auditorium, although rather long and narrow, was comfortable and more cosy than the vast auditorium of the Regal cinema across the road. It closed in 1960 and, like many ex-cinemas at the time, became a bingo hall – as can be seen from the photograph. The building was demolished in 1983 and its site is now occupied by the building shown below.

Royal Bank of Scotland, Vine Street corner, 2006. This was built on the site of the former Savoy cinema and the Westminster Bank (page 42).

Rear view of the Brookfield Hotel, High Street. This stood at the western end of the High Street and was demolished in 1937 to make way for an Odeon cinema. *(Uxbridge Library)*

The Odeon cinema, High Street, 1982. This cinema was by far the most modern and comfortable of the three built in the High Street between 1921 and 1938. It had 1,215 seats downstairs and another 622 in the balcony. As well as being the last to be built it was also the last to close, but before final closure it had been converted into a three-screen cinema. This did not stem the decline in attendance and it was closed in 1982. The building was demolished in 1984 to be replaced with yet another ugly office building – which did at least incorporate a replacement cinema.

The western end of the High Street, opposite the junction with Harefield Road, 1936. The Brookfield Hotel and the other buildings on the left, as far as the lorry in the middle distance, were demolished in 1937 to make way for the construction of the Odeon. (*Uxbridge Library*)

Town houses at the western end of the High Street, 2006. The handsome semi-detached pair of early nineteenth-century houses survived the demolitions to make way for the Odeon, as did the eighteenth-century building to which they are attached. They all have a Grade II listing but look out of place and forlorn among the modern buildings that surround them. In the middle distance is what remains of Fountains Mill.

The former Odeon cinema, High Street, 2006. This small building, now a fitness club, is attached to the large office block that can be seen behind it. It started life in 1990 as a two-screen cinema but closed in 2001 when the new Odeon complex opened in The Chimes shopping centre. On the extreme right of the photograph is the side of one of the town houses seen on the previous page.

The new Odeon cinema from the High Street, 2006. This multi-screen cinema was built as an integral part of the Chimes development. It has nine separate screens; the largest auditorium contains 418 seats and the smallest 195. There is one projection room that can service all nine screens simultaneously; they require only one projectionist between them. The cinema is comfortable with good sightlines and acoustics, but it lacks the style and opulence of the picture palaces of the 1930s.

Uxbridge Common, early 1900s and 2006. The common on the west side of Park Road is now only 15 acres in area but before the Inclosure of Hillingdon Parish in 1819 it was very much larger (page 7). It was then 4 miles in circumference and occupied both sides of Park Road, including all of what is now Hillingdon House Farm. A contemporary account of the Inclosure laments that 'Much of the enjoyment of this remarkable spot is now destroyed by the inclosure of nearly the whole. A measure which while it may have brought some pecuniary advantage to is promoters cannot but be viewed by every liberal mind as a serious injury to many poor families and a great detraction from the beauties of the surrounding scenery.' While this is undoubtedly true some consolation can be gained from the fact that Uxbridge did at least retain some of its common; most parishes lost them completely.

Swimming pool, late 1930s. The open-air pool was first opened in 1935 on part of the site of Hillingdon House Farm. It was initially closed to the public in 1986 but opened spasmodically on a few later occasions; it has now been closed for several years and heavily vandalised. Its principal five components (the pool, north fountain, south fountain, pavilion and entrance buildings) were each considered to be of special architectural or historic interest and were given Grade II status in 1998. It was built in a Modern style and is the only example of a twelve-sided 'star' swimming pool in the country. (*Uxbridge Library*)

The rear of the swimming pool pavilion, 2006. The pool is no longer accessible to the public but this has not prevented the entry of vandals who have done extensive damage to the buildings. Its Grade II listing preserves it to some extent, and proposals have been made for its refurbishment and the construction of an adjacent indoor pool in time for the 2012 Olympic Games.

Uxbridge Show, 1936. The first show was held in 1909 and it became an annual event that took place on August Bank Holiday Monday. From the 1930s it was held on part of Hillingdon House Farm but a series of wet Bank Holiday Mondays in the 1950s led to its abandonment. It was revived in 1966 as the Hillingdon Show and in 1986 became the Middlesex Show. Because of declining attendances it has not been held in recent years. *(Uxbridge Library)*

Hillingdon House Farm, 2006. The land which adjoined the parkland of Hillingdon House (page 99) was all originally farmed. It was bought by Middlesex County Council in 1931 and remained largely undeveloped until it was handed over to the tender mercies of the local council in the 1960s. Since then the edges have been nibbled away and in 1996 it was threatened by the construction of a Movie World theme park and studios. The plan was put forward by Warner Brothers with the active support and encouragement of Hillingdon Council, but it caused such public outrage that the company was forced to abandon its proposals. Soon afterwards political control of the council changed hands.

Fassnidge Recreation Ground, 1936. Sidney Fassnidge, a local builder, lived at The Cedars in the High Street (page 101) with his wife Kate. The Cedars had a large garden stretching down to the River Frays and the family also owned a field on the other side of the river. When Sidney died in 1926 his widow presented the field to the local council, to be laid out as a recreation ground in his memory. *(Uxbridge Library)*

A plaque in the recreation ground recording its origins.

6

Churches

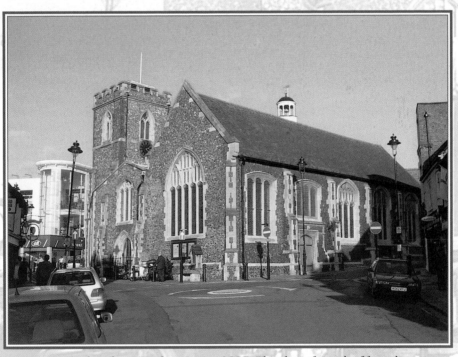

St Margaret's church in Windsor Street, 2007. This dates from the fifteenth century.
It is by far the oldest church in the town but was not originally the parish church;
when built it was a chapel of ease of St John's, Hillingdon, and came under the
jurisdiction of that church. It occupies a triangular site and is most unusual in not
having so much as the vestige of a churchyard. It is hemmed in on two sides by the
road and almost completely obscured on its north side by the absurdly close proximity
of the market house. Although still in occasional use for services, its main use today is
as a meeting place named The Nave.

St Andrew's church, Hillingdon Road, 1906 and 2006. 'Change and decay in all around I see' may be generally true, but seldom for an Anglican church – so it is unsurprising that the two external views of St Andrew's (and also the other Anglican churches depicted in this book), as distinct from its surroundings, look identical. The church was built in 1865 by a local builder with local bricks to a design of Giles Gilbert Scott; it was originally the parish church of Hillingdon West. It is not considered to be one of Scott's better designs and opinions of its architectural merits differ, but it is impressive in its way and an undoubted local landmark.

St John's church, Uxbridge Moor, 1978. This looks more like a non-conformist chapel than an Anglican church. It was built in 1838 to cater for the expanding population of Uxbridge Moor but is no longer in use as a church. After its deconsecration in 1993 it was adapted for office accommodation, but the external appearance has not been affected. *(Uxbridge Library)*

An interior view of St John's church, 1930s. *(Uxbridge Library)*

The Friends Meeting House, early nineteenth century (from a drawing in *The History of Uxbridge* by Redford and Riches, 1818). The Society of Friends (Quakers) had formed a group in Uxbridge by 1638 and the meeting house shown here was built in 1672. It was altered in 1817 to become the meeting house shown in the lower photograph, still in use by the Quakers. Both buildings show the simple pattern of a typical Quaker meeting house.

The Quaker Meeting House, Friends Walk, 2006. Although little changed, it is now completely surrounded and overwhelmed by modern developments.

Old Meeting Congregational church, Beasley's Yard, 1967. According to the original plaque on the wall of the tower the building dates back to 1716, but it was mostly rebuilt in 1883. In 1962 the members of Providence Congregational church (see below) united with the congregation of the Old Meeting House and the building was renamed Uxbridge Congregational church. This fact is recorded on the board on the tower that was placed over the original plaque. The building ceased to be a church in 1972 when services were transferred to Christchurch.

Watts Hall (formerly Old Meeting House), 2006. The building remains substantially unchanged but it is now used as office accommodation. The new name relates to Isaac Watts (1674–1748), a prolific writer of English hymns, many of which are still current – such as 'O God our help in ages past'. The original plaque is still in place on the tower.

Providence Congregational church, The Lynch, early 1930s. The building dated from 1796 and the classical frontage was added in the late nineteenth century. By the 1950s the congregation had so declined that in 1962 they amalgamated with the Old Meeting House, which then became the main Congregational church. With the threatened redevelopment of the town centre the church soon became derelict and it was demolished in 1969. Grainge's car park is now on the site. *(Uxbridge Library)*

Former Wesleyan Methodist chapel, New Windsor Street, 2006. The building dates from 1847 and was used by the Methodists until 1930 when the congregation moved to their newly erected Central Hall. It was then used as a Masonic hall for many years but has since been converted into flats and renamed Newland House. This involved the removal and replacement of the gothic-style windows at the front, although its origins as a non-conformist chapel are still very apparent.

The Methodist Central Hall on the corner of Park Road and the High Street shortly before its opening in 1930. Apart from its use for services this large building on a prominent site was used for a number of public functions. It was demolished in the early 1970s and the Uxbridge congregation merged with that of the United Reformed Church at Christchurch, which itself had resulted from a merger of the Congregational and Presbyterian churches. The board outside the church proclaims that it is 'The Church for Everyman', and that on Sunday 14 September there would be a 'Procession of Witness from the Old Chapel'. (*Uxbridge Library*)

Offices at the junction of Park Road and the High Street, 2006. This office block was built on the site of the Methodist Central Hall and was designed to blend in with its surroundings, all too rare in Uxbridge. The design is clearly based on that of the Hillingdon Civic Centre just across the road.

Another view of the Central Hall with the war memorial in the foreground, early 1950s, and the war memorial and St Andrew's Gate entrance to RAF Uxbridge, also early 1950s. There is some dispute over whether this is a war memorial or a peace memorial. It was erected in a prominent position in 1924 soon after the end of the First World War. Unlike most such memorials no names are inscribed on it. It was removed in 1972 and re-erected in the old burial ground in Windsor Street. In the lower picture and behind the memorial is what had originally been the entrance to Hillingdon House with the lodge house (since demolished) to its left (page 97). *(Top photograph Uxbridge Library; bottom photograph D. Rust)*

The St Andrew's roundabout underpass, 2006.
The construction of the roundabout to give access
to the new relief road at its junction with Park
Road and the old High Street involved the
destruction of the Eight Bells (page 97) and the
removal of the war memorial. Pedestrians now
have to make their way through a number of
murky tunnels in order to cross the road.
The smaller of the two plaques at the entrance to
the tunnel records that it was close to the site of
the war memorial.

The war memorial in the old burial ground in
Windsor Street, 2006.

The former Primitive Methodist chapel, Lawn Road, 1998. A Primitive Methodist congregation was established in the 1860s and opened this neat little building, typical of many non-conformist chapels, in Lawn Road in 1876. Meetings were held there until 1957 when the congregation merged with the Wesleyan Methodists at their Central Hall. The chapel and the adjacent corrugated iron building – a later and unfortunate addition which partially obscures the chapel – are now used as part of the Tara Kindergarten. (*B. Shorthouse*)

Lawn Road, 1998. The front of the former Primitive Methodist chapel is on the right and in the middle distance is the presbytery of the Catholic church. These are now separated from each other by a wall and a busy road. Before the redevelopment Lawn Road continued past the chapel and the presbytery and joined the High Street. (*B. Shorthouse*)

Christchurch, Redford Way (off Belmont Road), 2006. This belongs to the United Reformed Church, formed originally from the union of the Congregational Church of England and Wales and the Presbyterian Church of England that took place in 1972. Locally in Uxbridge the Methodist congregation from the Central Hall also joined the church, so the congregations from what had historically been four separate non-conformist churches were brought together under one roof. Christchurch itself is an attractive brick building with an unusual pyramid-shaped roof; it opened in September 1972. Inside there is a large meeting hall, which although primarily intended to be used for church functions is also available for other community activities of a suitable nature. In addition it has some ante-rooms that can be used for smaller meetings.

The Roman Catholic church of Our Lady of Lourdes and St Michael from Bassett Road, 2006. The church opened in 1931 to replace an earlier corrugated iron building in Lawn Road established in 1892. When built it was in a purely residential area with ready access from all parts of the town. The relief road put an end to this in the early 1970s and the church is now cut off from the south by the Uxbridge Wall. On the north it is dominated by the car parks and tower blocks of The Pavilions. The residents of this road and of Lawn Road were effectively cut off from the centre of the town by the redevelopment. *(Bottom photograph B. Shorthouse)*

Two views of the Roman Catholic church from the relief road. The church and the adjoining presbytery are now completely surrounded by modern developments.

7

Public Houses & Inns

The Swan and Bottle, early 1900s. This attractive inn, first recorded in 1761 and standing at the western extremity of Uxbridge, is situated between the River Colne and the Grand Union Canal. Historically the river formed the boundary between the counties of Middlesex and Buckinghamshire. It derives its odd name from two predecessors, The Swan and The Bottle.

River Colne from High Bridge, early 1900s. The view is probably to the south as neither the Swan and Bottle nor the Denham Lodge Hotel that stood on the banks to the north of the bridge are apparent.

The Denham Lodge Hotel, 1930s. This stood across the river from the Swan and Bottle and was therefore in New Denham, Buckinghamshire, rather than Uxbridge, Middlesex. It had started life as a private house and was converted to a hotel in 1945. It closed in 1962 and was replaced with the large block of flats seen in the next photograph. (*Uxbridge Library*)

Swan and Bottle, 2006. The pub has changed little in the last 100 years, which is more than can be said of its surroundings. The large block of flats that replaced the Denham Lodge Hotel can hardly be said to enhance the scene.

The Treaty House, early nineteenth century (from *The History of Uxbridge* by Redford and Riches, 1818). This building, which still exists, is the remaining wing of a much larger sixteenth-century mansion that had at one time been the home of Sir John Bennet. During the English Civil War it was known as Place House and was occupied by a Mr Carr; in 1645 it was chosen to be the meeting place of delegations from the Royalists and Parliamentarians with a view to signing a peace treaty. This came to nothing, but the house thereafter became known as The Treaty House.

The Crown and Treaty House, 2006. The Treaty House eventually became a public house, now known as the Crown and Treaty. The large oak-panelled room where the two opposing sides are reputed to have met during the Civil War still exists. This panelling was sold in 1924 and installed in an office in the Empire State Building in New York. However, it was reinstated to its rightful and more appropriate place in 1953 as a coronation gift to the queen.

The Falcon, 1967. All the buildings seen here date from the eighteenth century or earlier but the original Falcon Inn was in fact in the building (now the Nonna Rosa restaurant) on the left. In 1924 the licence was transferred to the adjacent building, which had previously been two semi-detached town houses. The building to the right of the Falcon had suffered the indignity of having its bottom half knocked out to accommodate a car showroom and petrol pumps.

The former Falcon Inn, 2006. All the buildings seen in the previous photograph remain and the building that had been occupied by Locomotors has been considerably improved by the replacement of its lower frontage. In 1984 The Falcon had been renamed The Continental. It then became a 'gentlemen's club', although whether the clients were gentlemen and it was really a club remain moot points. It has since become a restaurant.

The George Hotel and Inn, early 1900s. This building was on the north-east side of the High Street just to the south-east of Belmont Road. It dated from the sixteenth century but had been much altered over the years. In 1645 it was used as the headquarters of the parliamentary delegation that was discussing a possible peace treaty. (*Uxbridge Library*)

The George Hotel, *c.* 1950. The frontage of the hotel was extensively modified in the 1930s to give it a more impressive appearance. It closed in the early 1960s and after remaining empty for several years was demolished to make way for the parade of modern shops shown on page 56. (*Uxbridge Library*)

The Queen's Head, Windsor Street, 1950s and 2006. The plaque on the wall reads as follows: 'The earliest documented evidence of a public house on this site is 1544 but it is more likely that it dates back even further. It has been known as "The Axe" presumably at the time of Anne Boleyn's beheading, "The Angel", "The Jolly Ostler", "The Hostelry" and then "The Queen's Head" to commemorate Anne Boleyn, who is depicted in our pictorial sign today. Unusually the pub had its licence taken away in the early 18th century for around 25 years and it disappeared from records until 1769 when it was part owned by the Revd Thomas Millway and it is possible that it may have been used as a rectory. The fact that an underground passage linked the pub to St Margaret's church opposite lends weight to this theory. The Queen's Head has undergone various structural changes having had a stable yard and three separate bars and the pub frontage has had various numbers of windows and stable doors to suit its various owners and use at the time. In 1966 the Queen's Head was hit by an arson attack. Fortunately there were no serious injuries and it reopened that year in its present layout.'

The Three Tuns, High Street, 2002. This is the only survivor still in use as an inn of the fifty or so coaching inns that once lined the High Street. It is a timber-framed building dating from the sixteenth century to which has been added a modern frontage. The entrance to the coachyard at the right has some interesting old timbers. It and its neighbours to the left and right, notably the former King's Arms, form a group of Grade II listed buildings.

The King's Arms, High Street, 1950s. Like the Three Tuns, its near neighbour, this old coaching inn dated from the sixteenth century. It closed as an inn in the 1960s and for a short time, rather surprisingly, became the Uxbridge Gardening Centre. This did not last for long and it is now used as an employment agency. (*Uxbridge Library*)

The former King's Arms, 2006. The building mercifully survives in something like its original form, but it was badly mutilated when the downstairs frontage was changed to a style aptly dubbed by Ken Pearce as 'Kentucky Fried Tudor'.

St Andrew's church and the Eight Bells, early 1900s. The pub predates the church and St Andrew's does not have a peal of eight bells. The name in fact relates to the peal of St John's, Hillingdon, about half a mile away at the top of Hillingdon Hill. The pub was demolished in about 1970 to make way for the construction of St Andrew's roundabout and the relief road. A modern view of this scene is on page 76. (*Uxbridge Library*)

The Eight Bells shortly before demolition, 1960s. (*Uxbridge Library*)

The Wellington, Vine Street, 1967. This pub opened in the 1830s and was named after the Duke of Wellington who was the prime minister at that time. It was demolished soon after this photograph was taken when Vine Street was widened.

Site of The Wellington, 2006. The pub stood in the open space between the flats on the left and the office block on the right. The offices are known as Wellington House.

8

Private Houses

Hillingdon House, *c*. 1900. The caption 'Hillingdon Park' refers to the extensive parkland around the house, which also gives its name to Park Road. The original house was built in 1617 and rebuilt in 1717 for the last Duke of Schomburg. He was an argumentative British army commander of German origin who was said to have quarrelled with everybody except the enemy. This house was destroyed by fire in 1844 and the present house was built on its site. At the time of this photograph it was occupied by the Cox family who were prominent bankers in the nineteenth century. It was sold to the Government in 1915 and it and its extensive grounds are now part of RAF Uxbridge. (See title page).

Southern entrance to Hillingdon House, early 1900s. This is at the junction of Park Road and Hillingdon Road opposite to St Andrew's church. *(D. Rust)*

The former entrance to Hillingdon House, 2006. The gateway is still identifiable but it is no longer in regular use as an entrance to the RAF camp.

The Cedars, *c.* 1930. This is a handsome eighteenth-century house and one of the few that survive in the High Street. At the time of this photograph it was the home of Mrs Kate Fassnidge, the wealthy widow of Sidney Fassnidge. She was a public benefactor who had already donated the Fassnidge Recreation Ground to the public. When she died in 1950 she left the bulk of her money and The Cedars to set up a trust for the benefit of the elderly people of the town. However, she was not well served by her legal advisor, and it was many years before legal matters could be properly sorted out. *(Uxbridge Library)*

The Cedars, 1998. Superficially the house itself looks much the same but it is in a poor condition and not maintained as well as Mrs Fassnidge would no doubt have wished. At one time the trustees even lodged a planning application to demolish the Grade II listed building. Their latest proposal is to erect a block of flats in what is left of the garden, and with the proceeds refurbish the house and build a new hall as a meeting place for the Uxbridge Old People's Welfare Association. *(B. Shorthouse)*

The Cedars and Old Bank House High Street, 1967 and 2006. Comparison of the two photographs shows how little of the original High Street frontage remained after the demolitions in the early 1970s.

A rear view of The Cedars, 2006. This is all that remains of the large garden that once went down to the River Frays and thence by a bridge to the Fassnidge Recreation Ground across the river. It is proposed by the trustees of the Fassnidge Trust that a block of seventy-six flats should be built on this site.

The Cedars roundabout, 2006. Most of the area seen in the photograph was the garden of The Cedars until it was swept away in 1970 to make way for the relief road. It has been said that if Mrs Fassnidge knew what happened after her death she would not simply be turning in her grave but would be performing somersaults.

Park Lodge, Park Road, 1950s. This large house dated from the eighteenth century. In the early nineteenth century it was the home of John Chippendale, a local benefactor whose name is now remembered in Chippendale Way which joins Park Road at this point. It later became Park Lodge School, a private school for boys and girls. The school closed in 1960 and the house was demolished soon afterwards. (*Uxbridge Library*)

Park Road Day Nursery, 2006. The nursery on the corner of Park Road and Chippendale Way was built on the site of Park Lodge. The large cedar tree in the grounds is the only evidence of the existence of a substantial house on the site.

The Red House, High Street, 1967. This house opposite the Odeon cinema dated from the sixteenth century and the attractive red brick front which gave it its name was added later. At the time this photograph was taken a contemporary building to its left had already been demolished, and it was not long before the two buildings seen here also disappeared.

Site of the Red House, 2006. The only thing that these buildings have in common with what was there before is that they are also constructed from red bricks.

The Chestnuts, Honeycroft Hill, 1930 and 2007. This eighteenth-century house was the home of William Wilberforce between 1824 and 1826. He was a philanthropist and reformer notable for his efforts to abolish slavery within the British Empire. The two views give the impression that the house has not changed over the years, but it was extensively rebuilt for conversion into office accommodation in the 1970s and little of the original building other than the front façade remains. *(Uxbridge Library)*

9

Cowley

St Laurence's church, Cowley, from the south-east (from a drawing by D. Moule in *Picturesque Middlesex*, 1904). The church is the smallest medieval parish church in Middlesex and dates from the twelfth century. The bell turret and spire which do so much to enhance its appearance were added in 1780. Cowley is a small parish in its own right which historically covered some 300 acres. It is completely surrounded on all sides by the parish of Hillingdon and does not share a boundary with any other parish. Nor is this its only peculiarity as it consists of several areas completely detached from each other, only two of which are of any significant size (see the map on page 6) and in a manner that defies description. Apart from this some of the village of Cowley was actually in the parish of Hillingdon. As Walford in his *Greater London* (1883) remarked, beating the bounds of the parish could have been no easy task! Under the Divided Parishes Act of 1882 eight of the smaller detached portions of the parish were transferred to Hillingdon. Before the redistribution there could have been few if any other parishes in England with such strange boundaries.

Cowley church from Church Road, 2006. The appearance of the church remains, giving every impression of a small country church remote from anywhere. Sadly this is not the case: it is now surrounded by suburbia.

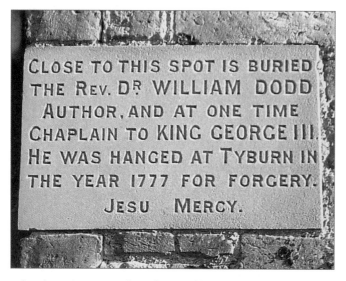

CLOSE TO THIS SPOT IS BURIED
THE Rev. Dᴿ WILLIAM DODD
AUTHOR, AND AT ONE TIME
CHAPLAIN TO KING GEORGE III.
HE WAS HANGED AT TYBURN IN
THE YEAR 1777 FOR FORGERY.
JESU   MERCY.

An inscription on south wall of Cowley church commemorating Dr William Dodd. Dr Dodd was a well-known cleric of the time who, despite having a considerable income, fell hopelessly into debt. He forged a cheque for £4,000 in the name of one of his former pupils and, although he refunded the greater part of the money and was forgiven by his pupil, was tried and sentenced to death. The jury in finding him guilty had added a strong recommendation for mercy. Despite this, the efforts of several prominent people (notably Dr Samuel Johnson), a thirty-seven-page petition signed by 23,000 people and the fact that Dodd was personally known to him, the king refused to grant a royal pardon. Dodd was hanged on 27 June 1777, thus becoming the last person in England to be executed for forgery. His body was taken to Cowley for burial because his brother Richard was the rector from 1771 to 1807.

The canal bridge and Shovel Inn, Iver Lane, early 1900s and 2006. The Brentford to Uxbridge section of the Grand Junction (now the Grand Union) canal opened on 3 November 1794. The bridge carrying Iver Lane over the canal and The Shovel date from this time and the name of the inn is a reminder that the canal was dug manually with picks and shovels. The two views, although separated by 100 years, are almost identical. But not quite: for reasons best known to the owners, the inn has now become the Malt Shovel. *(Top photograph D. Rust)*

The (Malt) Shovel from Iver Lane, early 1900s and 2006. In the distance are Cowley Lock and the lock-keeper's cottage – the first on the canal between Brentford and Uxbridge. The curiously shaped chimney on the right in the earlier photograph has been modified but its partner on the left of the later one is still original. *(Top photograph D. Rust)*

The packet boat from Paddington to Uxbridge from a contemporary drawing, 1801. Packet boats between Uxbridge (Cowley) and London (Paddington) were established in June 1801. They continued to pass regularly at stated hours every day for most of the year for the conveyance of passengers and parcels. However, the horse-drawn boats were slow, the distance covered was 23 miles and the passage soon became tedious. When the novelty wore off they were discontinued.

The Paddington Packet Boat, Cowley Road, 2003. This pub stands at the junction of Cowley Road with Packet Boat Lane and still commemorates the name of the packet boat service mentioned above. The quaint and unusual name has probably ensured that it has avoided the fashion to change long-established pub names to something considered more trendy.

Cowley station looking north towards Uxbridge, early 1900s. A branch of the GWR to Uxbridge (Vine Street) from the mainline at West Drayton was opened to passengers in 1856 and an intermediate station at Cowley opened in 1904. The station had two platforms with the main brick building including booking office and waiting rooms on the up side. A small waiting shelter was provided on the down side. The line was closed to passenger traffic in 1962 and the station was demolished soon afterwards. (*Uxbridge Library*)

Remains of the railway track, Cleveland Road, 2006. The site of the station remained undeveloped for many years but is now used for housing (Ruxley Close). To the north of Station Road bridge the cutting alongside Brunel University has been infilled, but a short length of track bed running parallel with Cleveland Road has been retained as a nature reserve and a short length of broad gauge track has been laid along it.

Railway bridge over Cowley Road, Cowley Peachey, 1934. The branch line from West Drayton to Uxbridge crossed the Cowley Road by means of this bridge. Its low height and the narrow road made it difficult for large vehicles to negotiate. This meant that all the buses between West Drayton and Uxbridge that used Cowley Road had to be single-deckers because the bridge was too low for double-decker buses. The large hoarding on the left is advertising 'ultra modern sun trap labour-saving houses' for £350 freehold, which was at that time about two years' wages for the average working man. *(Uxbridge Library)*

The site of the railway bridge, Cowley Road, 2006. So much has changed that it is difficult to believe that the two scenes were taken from approximately the same point. The bridge was demolished soon after the line was closed and the road widened shortly after that.

Cowley High Street, early 1900s. The view is to the north towards Uxbridge. On the right, almost obscured by the tree, is the Crown Inn. Most of the buildings seen in this photograph survive but it is no longer possible for children to play in what is now a busy road. *(D. Rust)*

Cowley Road, Cowley, 2006. The Grade II listed Crown Inn on the right dates from the sixteenth century but has been modified since the previous photograph. All the other buildings that can be seen also have Grade II listing, including the appropriately named Old House on the extreme left.

10

Hillingdon

The top of Hillingdon Hill with St John's church,
early 1900s. This gives a good impression of just how
narrow was the original road through the old village.
(Uxbridge Library)

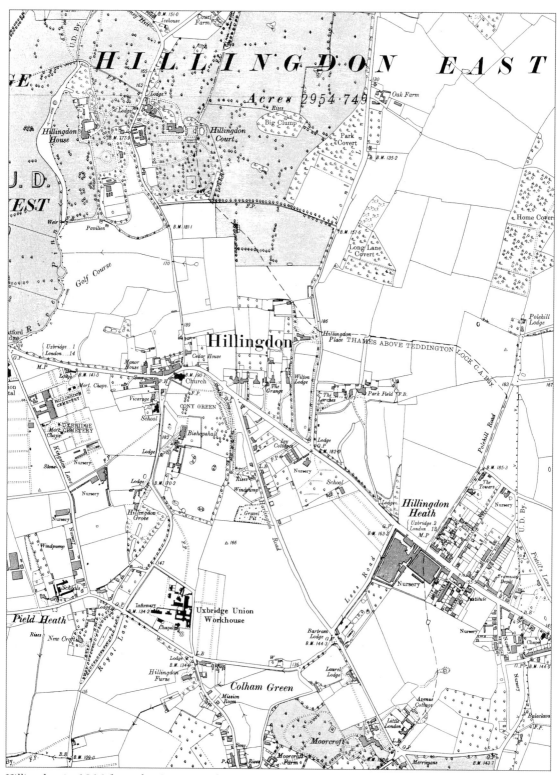

Hillingdon in 1916 from the 6in to 1 mile Ordnance Survey map. This is the eastern portion of the map shown on page 8. In 1916 Hillingdon was just a small village on the Uxbridge Road centred around the church. Much of the land to the north on either side of Vine Lane was occupied by the large grounds of Hillingdon House (page 99) and Hillingdon Court (page 123).

Hillingdon Hill, early 1900s. The view is up the hill with the gatweway to the cemetery on the right. Note the tramlines and the tram in the far distance. *(Uxbridge Library)*

Hillingdon Hill, 2006. The gateway to the cemetery is on the right and little appears to have changed. In fact the road seen here is the southern section of what is now a dual carriageway and houses line both sides of the widened road.

Vine Lane, *c.* 1920. The view is to the north, with the large grounds of Hillingdon House on the left and Hillingdon Court on the right.

Vine Lane, 2006. After the sale of Hillingdon Court in the 1920s houses soon appeared on the right (east) side of the road. The opposite side has been less developed because of Hillingdon Golf Course and the grounds of RAF Uxbridge.

Long Lane at the junction with the Uxbridge Road, early 1900s. The lane which runs from the Uxbridge Road to Ickenham is well named as it is almost 2 miles in length. It must have seemed even longer to travellers in the 1900s as there were very few houses along it. *(Uxbridge Library)*

Long Lane/Uxbridge Road junction, 2006. Houses started to appear along the length of Long Lane in the 1920s but they are set well back from the road. Most of the trees seen in the previous picture, or their successors, remain so they are not readily apparent. However, the road is now a busy thoroughfare and all its rural charm has been lost.

Hillingdon church and village in the early 1900s, looking east. Until Western Avenue (page 15) was opened in the 1930s the road through the village was the main route between London and Oxford. With the increase in motorised traffic and the narrowness of the road which curves round the church it was clear that something had to be done to remove the bottleneck. The church was the main stumbling block but was considered sacrosanct, so the only practicable solution was the demolition of all the old buildings on the north side of the road. *(Uxbridge Library)*

Hillingdon church and village, 2006. The scene is still attractive mainly because of the church and because the buildings around it on the south side of the road were not affected by the road widening.

Hillingdon village, early 1900s. The view is to the west and shows again just how narrow was the road through the village. All the houses on the right were demolished to allow for the road widening. The sixteenth-century Red Lion is on the left and thankfully survived. (*Uxbridge Library*)

The Red Lion at the junction of Royal Lane with the Uxbridge Road, 2006. In recent years the pub has been extended to become a hotel but the additions are discreetly hidden. Charles I stopped here during his flight in April 1646, which is how Royal Lane came to be named. The Red Lion and the adjoining buildings in Royal Lane form a group of attractive Grade II listed buildings.

Elm Tree Cottage, Royal Lane, early 1900s. This mid-nineteenth-century house acts as a good back-stop to the attractive group of buildings around the small green in front of the church. At the extreme right is what is now St John's church hall but was then a school. Further along the road on the left is the boundary of Bishopshalt. *(Uxbridge Library)*

Elm Tree Cottage, 2006. Nothing much has changed in the last 100 years but the parked car and the telephone box destroy the illusion.

Hillingdon Court, *c.* 1900. The mansion was built in the mid-1850s for Charles Mills, later Lord Hillingdon, the founder of the bank Glyn Mills and Co. (now a subsidiary of the Royal Bank of Scotland). When built it stood in large grounds that occupied much of the area between Vine Lane and Long Lane, and the Mills family also owned land beyond Long Lane stretching into Hayes. Charles Mills's son and heir (also Charles) was killed during the First World War and the house was sold by the family in the 1920s. The house and its immediate surroundings became a convent school. Some of its grounds were bought by the local authority to become Court Park and the remainder was soon covered with housing.

Hillingdon Court, 2006. A comparison of photographs of the building in the early 1900s and today reveals very little change. It is kept immaculately and has been very sympathetically converted to a school. It is now the ACS International School – a private school open to anybody who can afford the fees. Its previous name was the American Community School (hence ACS) but only a minority of the pupils are now Americans.

Bishopshalt, from a drawing of about 1890. This house in Royal Lane lies just to the south of the church. It was built in 1858 on the site of an earlier house that had belonged to the Bishop of Worcester – hence the name. It and its extensive grounds were acquired by Middlesex County Council in 1925, which tastefully modified the old building and added extensions to accommodate Uxbridge County School which had outgrown its premises in The Greenway in Uxbridge. The school moved to the new site in 1927 and was renamed Bishopshalt School in 1930. In all but name it was a county grammar school under the ultimate control of Middlesex County Council, but the then headmaster liked to give the impression that it was a public school. On his retirement it was renamed Bishopshalt Grammar School, but reverted to its former name when it became a comprehensive school in the late 1970s.

Bishopshalt School, 2005. Its appearance has changed little in the last 100 years.

Merriman's Corner, 1910. The point at which the Harlington Road crosses the West Drayton Road in the far south-east corner of Hillingdon Parish is known as Merriman's Corner. It derives its name from that of the early nineteenth-century house which stood at the south-east corner of the crossroads and which is seen here. This is said to have acquired its name from the Merry Man, a public house that had stood nearby. As shown later, each corner of the crossroads was occupied by a large house. *(W. Wild)*

Merriman's Corner, 2005. A block of flats and a petrol station now occupy the site of the house. Curiously the north-west corner of the crossroads has managed to survive unchanged and is occupied by Moorcroft, a large eighteenth-century mansion that has recently been refurbished to become office accommodation.

Moorcroft, 1800, from an illustration in *Hillingdon Through Eleven Centuries* by Rachel de Salis. There has been a house on this site on the north-west of Merriman's Corner since at least 1579 when, in a will of this date, Drew Saunders refers to his house called Morecrofte in the parish of Hillingdon. It is difficult to discern any link with the building depicted in the next picture but today's house of this name occupies the same site and presumably incorporates it.

Moorcroft, 2006. The present Grade II listed building is a large rambling mansion originally dating back to the eighteenth century but with many later additions. Throughout most of the nineteenth century it was a private lunatic asylum but more recently it has been an old people's home and a special school. It fell vacant in the 1990s and was sympathetically restored with the initial intention of converting it for office accommodation. It could not be let as offices and in 2006 it was being offered for sale as twelve houses and twelve apartments 'set in four acres of attractive parkland'.

The house to the north-east of Moorcroft. It is an early nineteenth-century house built on to a slightly older cottage set back at left. The house together with Moorcroft itself and other listed buildings close by, such as Vine Cottage, form an interesting group. It bears a superficial resemblance to the drawing of Moorcroft in 1800, but has fewer windows in its frontage.

The sixteenth-century garden wall of Little London, 2006. A house of this name stood at the north-east of Merrimans Corner but the only traces remaining are sections of its Grade II listed garden walls. Little is known about the house. A tablet in Hillingdon church records the death of John Walker of Little London in 1715. At a later date it was owned by a member of the de Salis family who also owned Dawley Court, which has led to confusion between the two quite separate houses. Until the mid-1990s the site was occupied by a horticultural nursery known as Little London Nurseries. Since then a small housing estate has been built and the name has been perpetuated: one of the roads is Little London Close.

Dawley Court, early 1900s. This house at the south-east of Merrimans Corner is frequently confused with Dawley House, a much more important building about a mile to the south in the parish of Harlington. It was at the south-east extremity of Hillingdon close to a point where the parish boundaries of Hillingdon, Harlington and Hayes meet. It stood on a triangular site bounded by Harlington Road, West Drayton Road and Corwell Lane. Its original name had been Gould's Green House but it was renamed when it was acquired by the de Salis family in the late eighteenth century. The de Salis family owned the manor of Dawley in Harlington but never lived there, and by then Dawley House had been largely demolished. It was probably because of this that they renamed their house – a matter for regret to local historians ever since. Sir Cecil de Salis, the last member of the family to live at Dawley Court, sold the house in 1929. It was demolished soon afterwards and the site is now covered with houses. *(HHLHS)*

The former lodge house of Dawley Court, Harlington Road, 2006. This is the sole remaining evidence of Dawley Court and when it was built, in the mid-nineteenth century, it stood at the southern end of the estate. Although attractive, it now has a road on either side and looks rather out of place.

ACKNOWLEDGEMENTS

As an eye-witness to what has happened to Uxbridge over the past sixty-five years I know the broad detail of events and have made my own photographic record of the changes. However, I do not have the detailed knowledge, particularly with regard to precise dates, of the two leading authorities Ken Pearce and Carolynne Cotton, whose books (noted in the Bibliography) have been the source of much of the information in the captions. Many thanks are also due to my wife Maureen, herself a native of Uxbridge, who has provided invaluable help and support in the compilation of this book. Also to Simon Fletcher and his colleagues at Sutton Publishing, with whom it is always a pleasure to work.

Sincere thanks are also due to the many other people who helped in providing information and photographs for inclusion in this book. This includes Carolynne Cotton, Gwyn Jones and Richard Daniels of Hillingdon Local Studies, Archives and Museum Service in Uxbridge Library, Flight Sergeant Carr of RAF Uxbridge, John Randall and Douglas Rust. The individuals and commercial organisations that provided illustrative material are acknowledged, where appropriate, in the captions to the relevant photographs. Where no acknowledgement is given the illustration is taken from my own collection. Finally 'acknowledgement' should be made to the councillors and officers of Hillingdon Council of the 1960s who did so much to make Uxbridge what it is today. Had it not been for them this book could not have been written!

BIBLIOGRAPHY

Cotton, Carolynne, *Uxbridge Past* (Historical Publications, 1994)

Hearmon, Carolynne (now Cotton), *Uxbridge: A Concise History* (Hillingdon Borough Libraries, 1983)

Pearce, K.R., *Uxbridge, Hillingdon and Cowley* (Sutton Publishing, 1995)

Pearce, K.R., *Uxbridge – The Changing Town* (Sutton Publishing, 1997)

Pearce, K.R., *A Century of Uxbridge* (Sutton Publishing, 1999)

Redford, G. and Riches, J.M., *The History of the Ancient Town of Uxbridge* (1818)

Skinner, James, *Around Uxbridge* (Tempus Publishing, 2004)

Skinner, James, *Hillingdon Cinemas* (Tempus Publishing, 2002)

Victoria History of the County of Middlesex, vol. 4 (University of London, 1971)